FEVER DREAM

FEVER DREAM/TAKE HEART
© Valyntina Grenier and Cathexis Northwest Press

No part of this book may be reproduced without written permission of the
publisher or author, except in reviews and articles.

First Printing: 2020

Paperback ISBN: 978-1-7342842-3-2

Cover art by Valyntina Grenier
Designed and edited by C. M. Tollefson

Cathexis Northwest Press

cathexisnorthwestpress.com

FEVER DREAM

Valyntina Grenier

Cathexis Northwest Press

IS THERE ONE CHANCE FOR THIS LEADEN VERSE	8
I CALLED BOTANY AS MUCH ABOUT THE HUMMINGBIRDS' LOVE	9
WE'RE POSSIBLY OUT OF CAKE	10
TRANSPARENT KITCHEN	11
UNDER TREES	12
LEAF N' BONE	13
ARE GRAMMAR'S ACTIVE SUBJECTS PASSIVE OBJECT'S EVERY SENSE	15
KITTEN AND CROCODILE	16
CREATION MYTH	17
IN OUR NOW	18
SEISMIC WAKE	19
CHILL	20
NEROLI	21
A WATER TAXI TO THE POEM	22
CAPILLARY ACTION	23

IS THERE ONE CHANCE FOR THIS LEADEN VERSE

Among the shadows of these pillars
I draw each capitol's ruined shape
a plump heart donned w/ a crown
the curve of your cheek
the gesture in your eyes

The sun hides our shadows
I lift your forefingers
to my forehead
I kiss
your wrist

I gesture and follow
under trees

I pull out a needle
and a spool of thread
to sew the straps across your slippers
while you sleep

I CALLED BOTANY AS MUCH ABOUT THE HUMMINGBIRDS' LOVE
as a human equivalent

Poor history
leaving altered notions through tanning

Intoxication
specifically ancient arts headed toward the gravitational pull usher beauty
into the moment

Attraction by token has a handful of chemicals
pleasure/ money/ a wormhole
that tubers, docile rams
and strangers mark

A marvelous imagination of aims shears some pardon history plays
Complexity and sophistication perfect how to refine our abilities' ore
so we are told

Making language our alchemist
transforms sunlight into accomplished beings
to manufacture

Nailing the astonishing trick
physics poisons
and delights

Rows and sheep power dreams
Trouble plants in our brains
to devise divisive recipes
Deadly poisons confect pedicures

Stirring in gratifying fact
mobility can't move/ locomote/ pray on
our tangled sleep
Strange

WE'RE POSSIBLY OUT OF CAKE
our brainstay

Tomorrow *earth* clear skies /w
degrees of intervention and departing no
spontaneously combusting selfblind

a chance of embitterment or cathexis

I feel it arriving something fast
making against some same
Sine and rain we condensate

Think of beads of mist gathering
along the outside of a water glass
Cool down against them and we do
have a pool
on some deeper hunter from go

TRANSPARENT KITCHEN

I bite each seashell gem between my teeth
to remind us we have bodies to please
each other with *Translucent buttons pop*
I lied about you not having my heart

Through a veil of beads I'm bound to one sleeve
My desire is thread to mend each hem
as minds and limbs w/ heat unjumble need
on the kitchen floor among shorn garlands

translucent buttons, scissors, ash and bone
"I have just now vacuumed," I lied That kiss
the first one upon our lips always just now

We sound the word poem as elision Poem
as half a foot We speak in poems like we
dream of our little columbarium

UNDER TREES

Her piano quickens me
w/ its great glass garbage
a reverie in all green

as the shallowest edge of the river
reflects through the canopy
to reach the sky

To fear nighttime
is no apostrophe

Monitors beam
marriage as the image of purgatory
homicide as the turning point
of love and desire
Gods fight over who is the god

Or god is breath
aspirating death

LEAF N' BONE

A wood hawk
standing on remnants of a life
empty nest fragments

Alone and the fodder is streaming
this was a logos
is
and under in
the distant rarefaction
of a frog bellow
fog bellow

Compression of a stag floating
downed from
a storm's rush
of current into wave
when up went some tree life

A hawk for the shackling
a suckling for hawk food
Wish is not for water
is of

basking midday
still
on the leaf and bone
life settles

Under claw
Un foot
Undulating breath
With it

some corrugation
some fold
A polar path
shadows light

Sum beam
via branchway
and pine

Beak needle
this kind of pain

inoculated into passing
the talon stretched
grasped a hummingbird and
can't fly

ARE GRAMMAR'S ACTIVE SUBJECTS PASSIVE OBJECT'S EVERY SENSE

As grasses conquer trees
origin demonstrates an outlandish new theory
artificial selection/ domesticated artifact/ a fake hybrid rose

is nature determining new forms and rules
deciding how well we'll be passed
w/ special round pills
A tiny pharmaceutical force felt the world round

Modification by dissent storms our reflection

Great has come to mean
absurdity rules space
Call the wild innocent influence to blow wilderness
planting trees
the wild's last default

Nature cum wiki-civilization
look apples/ pandas/ ocelots
ozone holes close

Futures will be strangely uncharted
Take place
a set of ever-expanding characters plants a world

Woven lives we scarcely suspect
default under civilization's white house

The metaphor is somehow
something happens outside simply
imagination's nature is also in

the kitchen
the brain
the holding up to look
inhaling smoke
the sway and the swagger

KITTEN AND CROCODILE

The soft nape of her neck
Woman and god
another rape another child

Why are there twins
Why does it thunder

We make this wind
its wrath

CREATION MYTH

He tells the child about the turn of the seasons
about seeds and how flowers rise

Her chest compresses against the bathroom sink
He gazes in his eyes jerking and panting lies
See it's raining he sighs

+

As I touch the bleeding swords of the sun
I say as I climb
through the scorching front seats
I'll drive

to the center of the sun
to save our lives

I leap stone steps
built into the curve of a tower wall
to find my self dreaming this life

I run screaming to my mother's side
away from a future
adolescent me

revolving slowly in a cave
w/ rays of light streaming
from my mouth nose and eyes

Fetal light like the tip of my toddler finger
translucent over the power light
on my great grandmother's electric organ

IN OUR NOW

Ordinary vision
is a hinge
crowded with flowers
busy/ multifarious
It feels like a city

In a quiet corner
a confusion of color and scent
is set to a railroad of insects
A carnelian dragonfly hovers to rest
after taking a turn on
our eye
Our eye?
All of the potential pollinators

Old roses
leave behind waded tissue
Inebriated anemones
are dining and humping
Trashed lilies lean in
Accept the invitation
into their throats of nectar
Afterward punch the air

SEISMIC WAKE

What planet am I from
dreaming of snakes

Does art educate emotions
Sacrifices are based on superstition

as corporations parallel Greek gods
sacrifice is based on analogs

Machines might imagine
the end of the world as a context

Siblings in a mine
day upon day before the quake

Held captive in the wake of the tsunami
determined to break free

Believe in the possibility of continuity
i.e. no end of the world

I shove a young rattler w/ the broom
They have to be coiled to strike

CHILL

Everyone is away this week as you seek
the nowhere everyone went to
summer's either-all highways
Remember community secrets
papyri stay

The chill either memorized shoulder blades
or you bought your other's obstruction
You said no last bold point
Bold, possessing emptiness
No one seeks substance

only closed space
light sealed solid against boulders/
caliche/ cacti No ticking day No void
Only you, finite thing

sober/ alone Your reason
made tight made no stillness
Your skins are sighted
only no one stopped
at your body

NEROLI

Lost echo
an arching sigh

Segments of citrus
your love is mine

I trace a helix over your sleeping eye

The tips of a trident
lift me

I float on my back
my arms spread wide

as I course out to sea
beseeching Chaos/ infinity
Help me
What is it

The embarrassment
the fulfillment

What

A sinister whorl

A WATER TAXI TO THE POEM

To reach the end of the atrocities we attend I pay the fair
                                       w/ pockets full of stones

Quit all violence
      quiet down
whisper
        quite down
Fear
    hear now here
comfy red fear
                                   We'll wake it in waves

CAPILLARY ACTION

Fish in bird flight
the whistle blows
one lonely boat
turns on the sea

My gratitude to the following in which some of these poems have appeared:

Neroli, a video valentine by musician and composer Aaron Embry
The Berkeley Poetry Review
Tulane Review
The Volta's Arroyo Chico

Notes: I selected the initial lexicon for "I Called Botany As Much About The Hummingbirds' Love," "Are Grammar's Active Subjects Passive Object's Every Sense" and "Ordinary Vision" from Michael Pollan's *Botany of Desire*. "We're Possibly Out of Cake" and "Chill" began as opposite emulations of a poem from Christopher Nealon's *The Joyous Age* and Pablo Neruda's poem "Poetry" respectively. The last line of "Are Grammar's Active Subjects Passive Object's Every Sense" is a nod to Laura Jensen's poem, "Bad Boats."

My gratitude to the following in which some of these poems have appeared:

The Berkeley Poetry Review
CatheXis Northwest Press
Spiral Orb
Tulane Review

Notes: I selected the initial lexicon for "Important Classes," "Pleasant Desultory Work" and "At the Front of the Perennial Bed" from Michael Pollan's *Botany of Desire*. The first draft of "Nice Work If" was written at the Squaw Valley Poetry Conference.

Lie down Remove this splinter We'll watch
flowers
Come here to me
be bold
We'll balance this freight on the rails
I'll wash
our winter jacket
phi 1. To mine
Press our palms
dress them
for rain
Already I
don't want to lose
this kind of consternation 1. *Constellation as all*
Knowing the feeling on

The present absence of the physical manifestation of our love has got me certain of one
I have chosen
this time to give
We'll switch
a gentle don't stop
on the hour

The splitters wash in The lumpers roll up I
have planned to kiss you along the chest once we transport this

I will be holding on to you

Until the conductor cries

All aboard to the last bodies

All aboard love All aboard

Pull down the window

Along about the sleepers I dash out this hello

Yes two women *on* or in Not against *beside*

Our bodies

Under one jacket in the rain reflexive as the wet streets

This is about emergence *Jacket this fortuitous arrival*

I've planned to reach out to press your palm

God play the Queen the best one for the tenth time
Bohemian Rhapsody shored against these tense degrees

Only me

This is we in proximity doing anything w/ out beginning

This is time for the long hand short

I've done with the old wish for rescue

I did not plan to kiss you on the cheek

Be certain of this, the antonym of indifference reeling at full rolling pitch
I am doing this all the way Come here to rest our fates
On one another's system of knowledge

Coming Current

The present absence of the physical manifestation of our love is making me
No others no
divided selves

Not a difference but my certitude

It is certain this physical position's consternation

I can do anything am doing anything right now

Always so earnest logging the moments to touch

I am going all ways *making*

A solid manifestation of our affection as a train perpetually arriving until we make the stop
Hold it this close the perpetual arrival of my hand in yours
My mouth
On you on

The hook is the flag with its bright feathers and food like the flag is a flair is the after the warning of a wave to end in the house but the curve to remembering the vacant fly bumping or floating un-curve to imagine the only way to in let me remember in when from a circle before again

No a point a nothing No yes just *beginning an end*

Ok that's a little out of line here's the hook that hook that hooks near the surface where wish and wonder skim the deep hoping for food in it a lake's place making that lake a space like Emily's window a thin pain between life and just this in *side the life* out side that flag on the flagpole flapping come sing to me speak to me the life you're remembering time tell me of it feel it making me of it blow in the wind

Yes where was circumference before a circle like a leaf shaped a lake like a fallen body an in the round ideology back again age pedaling for some one to stop this spinning come wave come wind with me stay here this time in wind back lash against flesh compacted the drain shows down the window the leaf keeps falling before the vacant curve before the flesh and food befog the love just the wonder

Slow down stop even Watch what *you're doing Yet* just keep going a *speed of refinement*

Its that that that we seek to refine we place words before time a vacant curve in the mother's belly but before this even a pane of glass to pack fresh words in before and after a love thaw *world-like* wordless light space before time or after the unknowable that drifts like a fetter bobs and curves un-catch able lupus into the lipase of a fish after a ruse floating on the water

These foyers reconnoitering for my substance fake eyelashes at the top of a flagpole flapping look at me authentic loved but under water there is a grill a forged force sucking all small things in and pulling the rest against the bottom until the current becomes so great bones break and flesh is compressed through

Cast me off Cast me off Set me down gently Hold me close

MORE ELSE

Yes into the floor under the baseboards and sunk into mud

Will you please will you please give me under the baseboards and sunk into mud cold and wet disturbing the earth failing and thinking all the same watering a dream or the water that I mean a coast one wonder some coast to be seen redwoods along cliffs with the ocean crashing

Red hooks among bottles a little tail feather and something that looks like food florescent pink Play-Doh and some mini maraschino cherry spheres cake cake cake pack pack pack into the hook and onto the water to out that life whole before water before under hear a place before words a sundry profession watered down gusts I digest the blank before time the wish before fish was staked out of water dreams dying before it that that there in that lake shaped like a fallen leaf so named and so named before the feather and food like the water was smooth and scales close to the rocks sang

Scrape me off Scrape me off I am fungal Scrape me off

Room cons womb

Rare sorrow from such spleen food
Yellow as urine chicken broth

fighter and feather
pillow of wonder

Fuel breaches a fire fence
We leap from climate dreams

Arrange a highlight where we sleep
The coyotes howl their watch along the sand
See the sea rise and sea foam shed from a rock

Crack each staff away from the beasts' faces
Form a welcoming
Interview the demagogues

How many cataracts will seep into a drizzle
before the flood waters rise

Our retribution patents cries
with alternative facts
from sunlit parched lips
skull dead skin and eyes
try not to try

Sirens come rushing our thug president
tethered to the front gates as one line as numbly
as a gale through fenestration bursts his yellow heart

One split ripe seed stills us to the cheek of an empty belly
Hunger cuts the sweet violence of a pot of gold

His letter had arrived with pros and coins to little fanfare
Dis was a god once, rapist god, seeking her out of heaven
Sweltering she humidifies heat
swell in such climates

I find myself set against self
twined to error bidding me to air
bellows through us
a pregnant platter of torn flesh
Bones rattle the wind

Bottles of glass scatter
and shatter through the wash
scoring white hot

Scalloped I reach for a length of rhyme
to tie around fingers to remind
two reminders with a bow to be kind
Too weak to self-soothe

another creature without legs
cracks a welt along my cheekbone

an oh well star burning in the wind for poems

Mineral tock of a stalagmite/
pendulum/ podium/ drop

to a frenzy of nonchalance
Just grab that mossy wedge

The derangement of tenderness

I make way with the weight of my cranium
for berries

Manacled priests and joyous children
wander about the path I tend

Times incise
Sharks crave the deep

Challenge eleven sills before the force of the flood
Swollen fleet of ministers hazardous from hell

don't fear yourself
the silken shadow of birth
your mothers' breath
Ololyga breaks from the outskirts to the square

We'll fine/
refine the subject
chain/ break/ make them

cast aside that foolhardy pulpiteer
to a cacophony of coyotes wild over one rat

AN OH WELL STAR

Baste me with salve
blast me into a gush of honey
wake me before my bones become hollow

Subject to hate bring on fever
I wallow/ sweat/ swallow
in sheets of mud

Screech a pitch to shatter the stars/
the gods Shards of cracked earth tumble
down a crest Lightning sinters my chest

Shallow fervor releases me from freedom
How can I feed a swell of hands over sand
rolling into a bawl

A later day lover feels the welt before my heart

My fevered bleat
to breach your guise
synesthesia/ my garments/ lungs
billow as a sail forced to the wind road

PLEASANT DESULTORY WORK

May afternoon suddenly appear
in manifold delights
the tung oil so innocent
acting on me
getting me to happen

Looking beyond the work bench
a same upside down book attempts the story
Human desires link destiny

Unconventional domestication
is something we do
something certain animals have done
success surprises
the seahorse and the frog

We figure how to heal, clothe, intoxicate and otherwise elate
As some ancestor mastered our wild cousins' prized wolves
values fold a sophisticated genome

We learn a great trick
ordinary credit
true volumes of ingenious sets
turn people into bees

Rich archives of DNA like sabers change beauty

the toxic unprepossessing
business of
remaking us

The perspective of the human looms
crowds with our species of harms

All the sacrificed ones wish
grander and probably designed
ideals of *tenderness*
didn't go unrecognized

In the cell where the eye is
lilies lend their faces
their favor shores
salacious pubic blame

AT THE FRONT OF THE PERENNIAL BED

At the front of the perineal bed there's a low soft forest of spikes

Look— dipped into that vibrating cloud's hairy irresistible bees
swimming with male and female genitalia

the floral point
they avoid pollinating themselves

Self-pollination is overdue
A stamen and pistol to stagger the times

Receptive among them sweets extend
with slender admittance to their first prying open

Pursed lips coil

Bees' desire is grafted in architecture
the around us surrounded in honeycomb

Hear the bees leeward
nosing like pigs through golden dust
rolling tenderly in a purple medusa

Transports of ecstasy are a projection
a magic beyond flower bee embrace
a designer drug deployed to drive lost work

Fine penises and prostitutes
deem themselves sugary nectars

I've fixed on the bee's eye

huh

peppers
and you reach for the smallest mini sweet bell
your cuts are so precise pretty biting
size

We get better at rationing
parceling out our lives
in sustenance bits

Look at the nest egg and find
how many

pieces can last to assay

Saw or sander
Sander
Saw
Hammer
Hammering
Hammerer

Shovel perhaps at earth and crag

New sprouts down there edit select all center
                                      something
I'm getting something

A cold oil
something like new sprouts or coals spoiled
No a cold oil

Chill of the wind
on burnt skin
The breeze for a moment

A car starts upstairs

Who

Ah a hoe

Paint scraper

face
so small it's more like a hill more like a hill
seems like a mountain to me

Heartbeat

It holds its form like a womb

Stick close to the teacher tendril of this multi-faceted-muse-walker-trail-seeking-sleep-organism-tossing-pebbles-into-the-pond

Cover your red wing muscle
so you don't have to fight as much for food

I'm about to raze babies I can tell by these insect cravings
They're all I can eat
munch munch
a worm
a horsefly
[insert list
of insects here]
Now I've got this fat baby that can eat twenty feet of earthworm plus in a sitting
Proof of pain
a family group of chickadees in here

Sander
Saw

The weight of his heart is almost imperceptible The rate of his heart
the wait
heart
imper

Here the males come with their pesky sap
stuck to the ass of my leisure pants

Grab that pollen and gestate little female cone
Keep it safe inside the flames

Nude buckwheat

The almost pitiable

spending this time
in silence
stillness' sound

light

saw or sander
hammer

floating at rest

See how we can spend this time peacefully
we feel
we feed

Ourselves

We can feed ourselves without warring

I like warning my feet on hot ground

The sun to bake
The sun to bake in
feed on
hop in
take its rays deep
through skin and in
warming our hearts

Hear
a man and a horse on the hill moving behind a pine
The pine
that pine
perfect rhyme

We seem so refined or not
direction for thought
the words sound and not
some that sing slant rhyme

O, that mountain these pines

Rock

I like those
non-color colors next to each other wrapped in
patterns on a form a

body

Two bodhis together

Many

Hammer
Saw or Sander

a life

Hear
a storm and a train and a child walking
through the brush
Mush mush mush go the twigs
and leaves into the mud
damp earth O
it is you I'm thinking of
How are those friends of yours

the girl who grew up above a liquor store
and her two best friends *young boys*
the trailer park next store

How are you
How's your new home
How's your loved one
I heard something about some toxic mold
I hope that's all dried up now and you're
Snuggling in

This is/ was/ is
your time too

and you   and you

and you
Do you see we are here now

NICE WORK IF

Saw or sander
sander/ saw
Hammer

hammering

Here
this place this porch the sun
new sap on a fresh cut

Bench

sander or saw

the sun

The wind
The trees
This is it now
too
This is you
your life your time your sun of an afternoon
couch in a dim room
poolside lounge chair or plastic swimming pool

Your time on a bench my time on a bench

Here
There's a blue jay
hopping around the base of a pine
a clear *some purple sky*

Who names the colors
Whose eye

The spectral ones

in black and white

IMPORTANT CLASSES

Fruit, flower and drug staple time
or another intimate stories each chapter
starts out
stops by
ventures far afield
for a brief perverse moment
of precious gold

Corporate engineers have reinvented love

People are nature telling ourselves what we call time has glazed across the galaxies

or a pathetic fallacy

It's a shame
even when the tenor changes
the gulf remains

Precious history paddles a canoe
An old "heroic" man emerges

Environmental morality
pays for transgressions
usually in coin

Disasters can't shake
how different aims
wrap us in the reciprocal web of

hope clothes us
From covers we'll look up
a little road
won't appear so alien and intimate

Design and desire
our knees and genius gaze
recklessly remarkably
unself-conscious at the mirror

SCORE SUSTENANCE

There is always already a war going on

all our dead
w/ all our little deaths

A lead heart exposed
as a chaff of grain packed in flesh

In the wake of two atomic blasts
an unknown number of hearts were made ash

The almost instantaneous expansion
violence as air

Mortals projectile
Waves incinerate

Here we are from a page
hanging in air

Have you heard
bombs going off

Shells scatter

In a spray of shrapnel
flesh becomes mist

Bones give off carbon-13

While for you

for me
our breath becomes mist
for all
for each one

gather

SCORE SUSTENANCE	8
IMPORTANT CLASSES	9
NICE WORK IF	10
AT THE FRONT OF THE PERENNIAL BED	16
PLEASANT DESULTORY WORK	18
AN OH WELL STAR	19
MORE ELSE	25
COMING CURRENT	29

TAKE HEART

Valyntina Grenier

Cathexis Northwest Press

FEVER DREAM/TAKE HEART
© Valyntina Grenier and Cathexis Northwest Press

No part of this book may be reproduced without written permission of the
publisher or author, except in reviews and articles.

First Printing: 2020

Paperback ISBN: 978-1-7342842-3-2

Cover art by Valyntina Grenier
Designed and edited by C. M. Tollefson

Cathexis Northwest Press

cathexisnorthwestpress.com

www.ingramcontent.com/pod-product-compliance
Lightning Source LLC
Chambersburg PA
CBHW051354070526
44584CB00025B/3761